Superstars
of the
CLEVELAND
CAVALIERS

by Annabelle T. Martin

AMICUS HIGH INTEREST ⬩ AMICUS INK

Amicus High Interest and Amicus Ink
are imprints of Amicus
P.O. Box 1329, Mankato, MN 56002
www.amicuspublishing.us

Library of Congress Cataloging-in-Publication Data
Martin, Annabelle T.
  Superstars of the Cleveland Cavaliers / by Annabelle T. Martin.
      pages cm. -- (Pro Sports Superstars (NBA))
  Includes index.
  Audience: Grade: K to Grade 3.
  ISBN 978-1-60753-767-0 (library binding)
  ISBN 978-1-60753-866-0 (ebook)
  ISBN 978-1-68152-018-6 (paperback)
  1. Cleveland Cavaliers (Basketball team)--History--Juvenile literature. 2.
Basketball players--United States--Biography--Juvenile literature. I. Title.
  GV885.52.C57M37 2015
  796.323'640977132--dc23
                                    2014044497

Photo Credits: Charles Krupa/AP Images, cover; Jonathan Bachman/AP
Images, 2, 16; Mark Duncan/AP Images, 5; AP Images, 6; Dick Raphael/
NBAE/Getty Images, 9; Bill Baptist/NBAE/Getty Images, 10; Rocky Widner/
NBAE/Getty Images, 13; David Maxwell/epa/Corbis, 14; Tony Dejak/AP
Images, 19; John Raoux/AP Images, 21, 22

Produced for Amicus by The Peterson Publishing Company
and Red Line Editorial.

Designer Becky Daum
Printed in Malaysia

HC 10 9 8 7 6 5 4 3 2 1
PB 10 9 8 7 6 5 4 3 2 1

TABLE OF CONTENTS

MEET THE CLEVELAND CAVALIERS

The Cavaliers started playing in 1970. Some people call them the Cavs. The team has had many stars. Here are some of the best.

AUSTIN CARR

Austin Carr was Cleveland's first star. He scored many points. Carr hurt his knee in 1974. He had **surgery**. But he came back strong. He helped the Cavs reach the playoffs three times.

Carr's nickname is Mr. Cavalier.

BRAD DAUGHERTY

Brad Daugherty joined the Cavs in 1986. He was a big player. He stood 7 feet tall. Daugherty could score. He made it look easy. He was also strong. He could grab **rebounds**.

Daugherty loves racecars. He even owns a racing team.

MARK PRICE

Mark Price joined the team in 1986. He was just 6 feet tall. But he made baskets. He was a great free throw shooter. He scored from near and far.

LARRY NANCE

Larry Nance could leap high into the air. He was a great dunker. His powerful jumping made him a great **defender** too. He could block shots. Nance played with the Cavs until 1994.

ZYDRUNAS ILGAUSKAS

Zydrunas Ilgauskas is from Lithuania. He stands 7 feet tall. Fans call him Big Z. Big Z could do it all. He scored. He rebounded. He blocked shots. He helped the team reach the **NBA Finals** in 2007.

KYRIE IRVING

Kyrie Irving was born in Australia. His dad played basketball there. Irving grew up to be a skilled player too. He hits three-point shots. He makes **assists**. Irving was named an NBA **All-Star** in 2014.

Irving loves acting. He was in plays in high school.

KEVIN LOVE

Kevin Love began his career with the Minnesota Timberwolves in 2008. Within a few years he was a star. Love scores points. He grabs rebounds. He joined the Cavs in 2014.

LeBRON JAMES

LeBron James is legendary. He is a 10-time All-Star. He left the Cavs to play for the Miami Heat in 2010. He won two championships there. But James returned to Cleveland in 2014.

The Cavaliers have had many great superstars. Who will be next?

TEAM FAST FACTS

Founded: 1970

Home Arena: Quicken Loans Arena in Cleveland, Ohio

Mascot: Moondog the Dog

Leading Scorer: LeBron James (16,483 points as of February 25, 2015)

NBA Championships: 0

NBA All-Stars: 15, including Austin Carr, Brad Daugherty, Mark Price, Larry Nance, Zydrunas Ilgauskas, LeBron James, and Kyrie Irving

WORDS TO KNOW

All-Star – a player named as one of the best that year

assist – a pass to a teammate who scores

defender – a player who tries to stop the other team from scoring

NBA Finals – the games played to decide the NBA championship

rebound – a ball that bounces away from the basket after a missed shot

surgery – treatment of an injury or illness inside the body by a doctor

LEARN MORE

Books

Birle, Pete. *Cleveland Cavaliers*. La Jolla, Calif.: MVP, 2014.

Labrecque, Ellen. *Cleveland Cavaliers*. Mankato, Minn.: Child's World, 2010.

Websites

Cleveland Cavaliers—Official Site
http://www.nba.com/cavaliers
Check player stats. See videos of your favorite Cavaliers.

NBA Hoop Troop
http://www.nbahooptroop.com
Follow your favorite basketball teams. Learn more about today's superstars.

INDEX